STAY STRONG Bitch

This book belongs to:

_____

I0529146

Color Testing Page

Use this page to test your crayons, colored pencils,
markers, gel pens, & more!

Blotter Page

If using markers, cut out this page & put it behind your coloring page to prevent bleed.

WITH A LITTLE swearing I CAN DO anything

YOU ARE awesome KEEP THAT SHIT UP

© Positively Delighted - PositivelyDelighted.com

I'M JUST WTF-ING MY WAY THROUGH LIFE

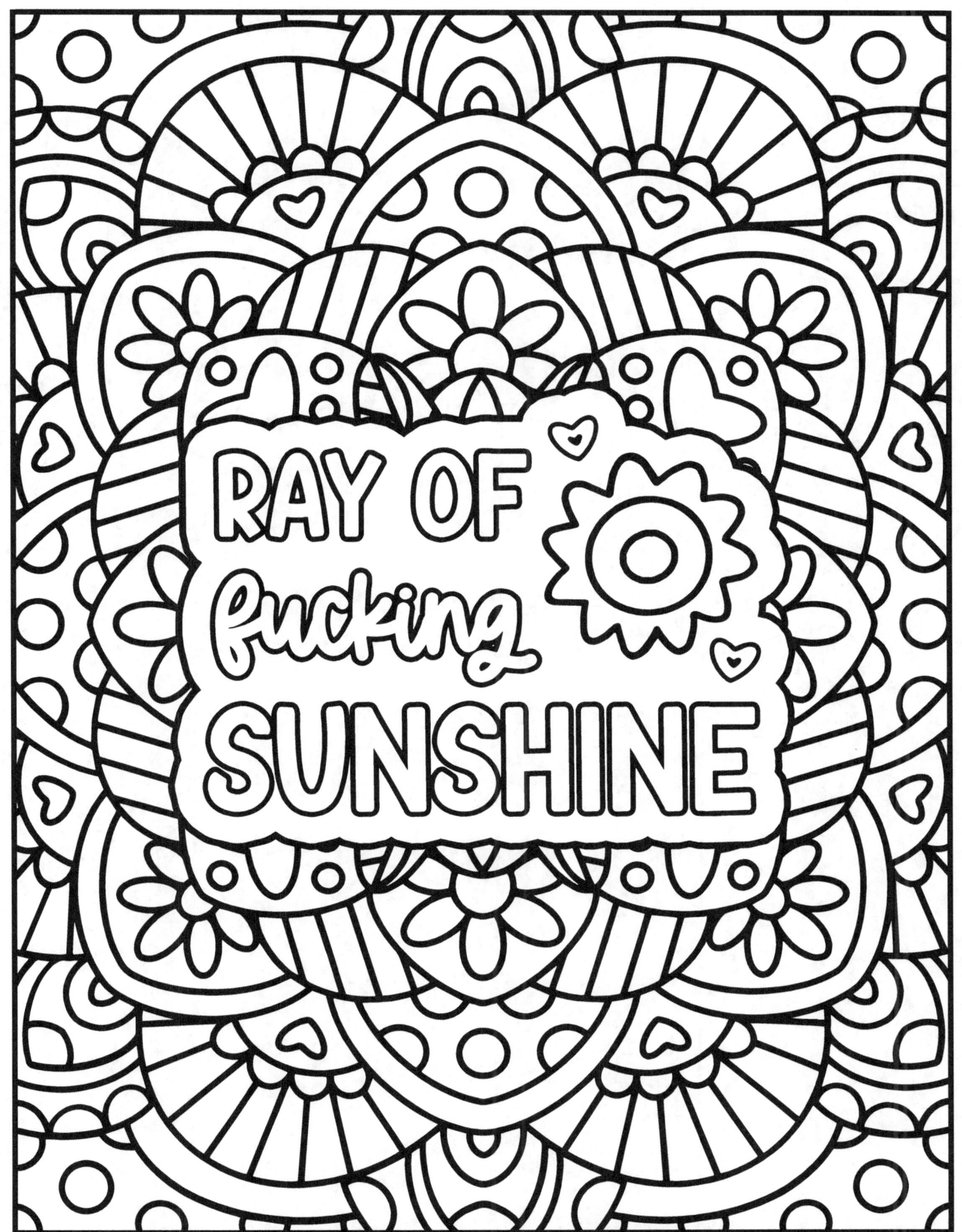

Beautiful
Intelligent
Talented
Creative
Hell of a woman

DON'T SWEAT
the small shit

I WAS LIKE WHATEVER BITCHES AND THE BITCHES WHATEVERED!

LIFE HAPPENS
swearing helps

FUELED BY *caffeine* SARCASM & *f-bombs*